DICING FOR PEARLS

JEREMY REED

DICING
FOR PEARLS

ENITHARMON PRESS 1990

First published in 1990
by the Enitharmon Press
40 Rushes Road
Petersfield
Hampshire GU32 3BW

© Jeremy Reed 1990

ISBN 1 870612 80 9 (paper)
ISBN 1 870612 85 X (cloth)

Set in Monotype 12 point Bembo (270)
by Gloucester Typesetting Services
and printed by
Antony Rowe Limited, Chippenham Wiltshire

Illustrations by Jean Cocteau

CONTENTS

For
Sarah Westcott

An auto turning redder and redder is a dizzy stain of madness on the ribbons and nets of tar that keep the countryside from flying away.

René Crevel, *Babylon*

LITURGIC

So often the word ascends vertically.
I am a man of the late century
inheriting dark.

      The drugs that have damaged me,
the thumbprints that have walked over my eyes
I see now as a deepening. Red boat
in the sun, together we might have journeyed
through light years. Known space as lucidity
angels point through.

In a wheatfield my words flower blue
like the sky-faced cornflower. I trust prayer,
like poetry, somehow gets through.
Breath activates so many syllables,
I expect books to dance
for the tune within them.

We are of the one stem,
life and poetry. The rose-thorn, the bud.
I hope in the end it means there,
in the undirected space I speak into
that's high and blue.

METABOLIC

The arc's irregular.
I'm ruled by feeding fear
with chemicals, little blue life-savers
regulating a just liveable calm.
I'm hooked, unable to get clear
of the panic generated by need –

15 in each pocket,
and paranoia leaving me alert
to being followed or a face
trying to get inside my head
and on bad days breaking out,
delirious, obsessed.

That time I thought the plane would crash
over the mosque in Baker Street;
I saw it occur, the red flash,
the detonative tear;
but nothing happened. I was in the park,
hallucinating fire in air.

I make a friend of imbalance,
it is a way of getting through.
15 in each pocket to help
modulate the speeded-up
film-shots that go straight through me.
Whatever's in there needs to stay.

Insider, outsider, I try
to work with my duality.
The drug, the fear, make poetry?
I've never known another way,
living on the edge of things,
trusting it will be O.K.

Brought to completion on the edge of space

he is awareness of himself without
embodiment, a continuity
of things achieved to be given away
to hands cupped in the asking.

What once was done has learnt to live for him,
the poem too has blue eyes and a face
we recognise, identity
questioning us to take it in
as a deer drinks the horizon

by readings of the wind. Blue pines, green sky,
he's nearer to this now – separation
was once a way of seeing, birds

stunned themselves on that mirror.
The angels have gone back into the world
instructing where the nerve-centres
are open to the seeded word's
appropriation – and again

the voice is carried. He's fulfilment now
in the still place the light once pointed to
while reading, writing, receptive
to how the force lifted him into space

and then returned him. And it's very clear
that partial beginnings were in themselves great,
before he grew to be his own guardian.

Music. Breathing of statues. Here a deer
startles at its enquiry in a pool,
takes up the note he found in autumn's cool
dispensation of apple, pear.
Great happenings are in the stars, and he

is read by a student somewhere
at a café table, imagining

not someone, but the arc of going free.

He lectures with his back to us.
Black-suited, head inclined towards his feet,
we never see his face; to turn about
would be to betray his subject,
and the diagrammatic model used
to instate thanatography
is relayed on strategically placed screens.

Mostly he talks. The audience
never question. Sometimes they're upside down,
feet on the ceiling – reverse perspective
of how they lived. We misread

life and stand death on its head;
the red exit signs are hardly visible
for smoke, and no-one ever leaves that way
to watch boats cross the river.

He speaks of adapting to a topos
that in time we'll assimilate,
the night-world compensating for the day,
though it gives nothing back.

We listen in the absent dimension.
The lecture ends. He walks away
into a blackout uncontested by
a voice, a shout.

We hardly see you now; the other you
depleted by internal scars,
an earlier, adventurous subject
is backlisted, seldom in evidence.
The cloud never shifts to reveal the inner blue
we hope is somewhere there
on call, blue of the first crocus
translucent in frost-silvered air.

We speak of you in the past tense,
editing what we recollect
as though you stood still, fish without water
because you've drunk the tank
and can't float free.

We think of your most secret years,
the nocturnal biography,
duplicities, the internal cyclone
that fetched you up in black alleys,
and finally at a wind-tower
on a stormy night when you broke;
the local doctor sedating you with morphine . . .

And now you're uncontactable,
out of town, composing nocturnes
to a new prelude? It will grow,
the reassurance that there's a way back,
a gradual strengthening, instructive voice,
taking you down the stairs towards
an open door. And there's no choice.

OASIS

A scarlet Maserati cuts a line
across a dust road. An immobilised windmill,
a sack-stashed granary,
and aerosoled on a wall – The Blue God
has gone away: a family
staring from a farm, thinking without speech

that language died so long ago
that now only are events, and they
are always somewhere else; a blurred montage
miraged on the air, an oasis
hanging in 3-D?
                    Above it,
                    a white star.

Chickens stab at the cinder
path. The army left a photograph
of a black hole,
a circular void.

The car accelerates again
lifting a dust cloud with no fire inside
to guide a people back to the most simple prayer
for words, abundant rain.

An emerald lives in the fern's heart. Still
shine like this pool in the valley
where a deer hallucinates.

Everywhere, molecular configurations,
the invisible pattern,
the lizard's discarded, rusty scabbard;
the fly's shivering constellation.

Birth was yesterday in a stone house, bees
and the bloody contortion
and the stones lifting to support flesh drawn

to exhaustion. It is someone coming,
breath and symmetry

and later the dust rising with thunder.

PUNCTUM

High-pointed mineral puncta – star-glitter:
the night and Rilke's *Elegies*
on a bedside table.

If there are reasons to withdraw I see
the day in flashbacks; you surprising me
with trepidation on your lip
at how little we elucidate
of feeling: one hand on your hip,

asking I translate it to imagery –
a windmill on a plain, bottle-green sky,
the concordance of emotion
following from there; two amazed

at being together on that blue plain.

A half-drawn red curtain. Rectangular
look-out on how the open page
leaps from the word to a simultaneous star.

I

A plain dotted with black and white horses,
necks arched, marbled with inky clouds
pacing magenta splashes with the wind.
Nearer field maples, clustering.

You remember the day to a detail;
a montage, and your nerves stretched; breaking-point
described by a bolting foal.

Later a shower throwing a fine net;
the pain in time hardening to a pearl,
an incoercible black grit.

II

Your face assimilated into space.
If I returned to that place in high wind
I'd see myself debating you
as you were then. Red scarf tied in your hair.
My intensity told me that you knew

I'd placed you amongst horses; lilac skies.
Today it's crocuses, saffron, blue tips
I study in passing. Cold-effulgence;

the feeling less approximate
like reading a poem in translation –
Rilke or Pasternak, the intimations
suggesting decreased tension, loss

of polishing the yellow apple's gloss.

FASHION

Its universal dictates catch the eye,
we're with it as it falls unconsciously,
its implants dominate the age –
art we can model as an extension

of who we are, mood-exchanges, a way
to register in flux, that tie's
cerise flame flicking free from a black suit,
the moment caught by the appreciative

as something in youth that won't come again,
the burning impulse never to grow old.
With her it's different, her bottom caught
in a violet crocus's fluted sheath,

her clothes pronouncing curves, the feminine
constant in its attraction, red jacket
offset by black stilettos, pencilled seams,
the street giving back to that beauty gold

light falling through flowering acacias.
Mostly the eye arrests detail –
a row of buttons, how a hat responds
to light and shadow in a face, and so

we look for visual precedents, the black
mode occupying half a century
from Juliette Greco to the street-wise
finds its individual corollary

in fifteenth century portraiture, a means
of celebrating the individual,
emphasising how different we are;
we looked like that. And it's a memory.

It is a means of resolving light-planes,
you standing in the green interior
of a pine kitchen, looking out at how
she sits writing at a garden table,
shaded by a white umbrella, the door
you stand in turning yellow-lime

from a leaf-flickery, blond luminous
sunshine – her involvement, not yours.

Inside, the visual compensations shift
your awareness, oranges grouped in a blue bowl,
a lemon, lime, things that Cézanne
might have arranged on a white cloth
find here their natural dispositions;
the radio's tuned to another continent.

Dark and light: you wouldn't change
their properties – the peeled orange is sweet,
a sharper taste of sunlight while
she strokes daisy-heads with her feet,
leaving you to rearrange
oranges, lemons, limes and then retreat.

LOST WORKS

I

A blue apple in a green bowl;
I have sung of transformations
through dynasties:
plum blossom snowing on the tongue
of a Chinese poet; an isotope
guiding a man through black deserts
in search of a line
that recedes with the horizon.
A prayer book open without words,
I have read silence to the hills
and not heard it return.

II

A blue peach in a red bowl;
I have heard the lost poems migrate
leaving as a legacy
madness, dust in the mouths
of singing men. Of Hölderlin.
The purple lords, grammarians
I served are gone.
                    Now I am free
to abdicate.

TWO HOPES

I

A green moon in a cobalt sky,
it is our starting point, a convex space
we have to landscape or leave blue

with unintrusive possibilities.
A bird sings but we don't admit
the Chinese brushstroke of a tree
as its placement. It is lighter now,
greener for moonshine clarity

and music leads impromptu,
spontaneously
in E.

II

A black sun targeted between
scarlet daisies, each radial
illuminated by surface-tension.
We're no nearer discovery
in remarking how the immediate
might open out,
potentialised.

Hope as it's contained in a fruit
is the lyric seed, blue-bright star
embedded in the tongue,
so sing.

THE ONE

You could be anywhere –
the wind snapping a black scarf in your hair,
a spine-split book of poetry
in a greatcoat pocket,
walking the winter streets of Manhattan,
or on a surf-thrashed beach in the Camargue,
hipbones pronouncing a black bikini,
Cap Ferrat, Biarritz, Copacabana –
always the same inimitable beauty,
followed but never turning round
to own to an identity.

I've searched for you through so many cities,
giving back what you offer me –
the gift of poetry,
words answerable to your elusive
neither-here-nor-there anonymity –
a face amongst the crowds,
mouth open to catch snowflakes, or naked,
emerging from a violet sea
to roll in a red towel. I sit and wait
for your appearance, that's more frequent now
in the advancing century.
I contemplate crossing the new threshold
with you – two pinpoints on the brink of space
running to meet the continuity . . .

Two I picked up off the crown of the road,
disturbing a peacock jewelling of flies;
an iridescent blue-green neck-choker
working the mine of the split skull, the eyes

were buttoned by bluebottles, not a sound
in the lane, the hedges frothed with bindweed;
the flipped one had internal injuries,
a gut fissure open, spilling red seeds;

my toe worked its body into the ditch,
a trench stuffed with last year's leaves, a warped boot . . .
Victims of fast cornering, white headlights,
they'd died in the black of the night, the hoot

of owls floating up from a ruined barn.
Boar and sow, I'd discovered so many
scutched by a tyre's chevrons; blue mole and rat.
I placed their bodies in a hollow tree.

Hedgehogs had dug into this territory
and surfaced in my childhood, one had strayed
into our woodshed and had wintered there.
The story went that one a badger flayed

had bitten back so hard its teeth blinded;
another sucked the udders of a cow.
They kill a viper by biting its tail,
lock tight, and leave the snake to die a slow

death on the ball of erect spines, and drag
their carrion back to underground lairs.
Their need to go out is the need to kill.
Their cautious gait's defiantly aware

they'll master all but the fox, badger, dogs;
sniffing through the brush, tracked by white moonlight,
alert to a fieldmouse's quick scamper,
the blood-quivering flit of a vole's flight.

THE SWAN
(after Charles Baudelaire)

I
ANDROMACHE, I think of you. The mirrored stream
which once reflected your heroic years
dehydrates to a trickle. History's
in dry-dock; berthed in a tangle of piers.

As I was crossing the new Carrousel,
the notion of things lost became a truth;
old Paris had so quickly disappeared
I was reminded of my vanished youth.

Round by the barracks, the town's vertebrae
were visible: its roughed-out capitals,
builder's debris, bric-à-brac, fireweed, grass,
smashed columns devastated by vandals.

And on the site of a menagerie,
I saw one morning creeping to my lair
in that first pink light when a roadgang starts
with drills and sledge-hammers to smash things bare,

an escaped swan, broken out of its cage,
flip-flap on the pavement with webby feet,
and soil its spotless plumage on the ground,
its fractured pinions attempting to beat,

before it jabbed its beak into the dust,
thirsting for streams, blue lakes, its instinctive
places of homing, fast electric storms;
the drenching sparkle that will have it live.

The bird seemed the symbol of Ovid's myth,
stretching its convulsive neck to the sky,
snake-like, accusatory, biting the air;
reproaching the gods with the truth *we die.*

II

Paris changes; my black mood's permanent.
New highrises, penthouses, can't atone
for straggling suburbs, scaffolding, raised blocks:
my memories weigh on me like a stone.

Here by the Louvre, I feel the irritant
oppressive image of the swan; its mad
gestures of a delirious exile
trying to turn up a culture gone bad,

and of you, Andromache, torn from the bed
of your great lover: winded like a slave.
Pyrrhus stamping on you, Hector's widow,
crouching wide-eyed beside an open grave:

and you Jeanne Duval, tubercular, sick,
I think of you lost in the opaque fog,
tramping the mud, searching for Africa's
luxuriant palms, harassed by a dog.

I think of losers, the ones left behind
by time's remorseless boot, those who lie down
to suck a wolf's tits, men consumed by grief,
public orphans who like dead flowers turn brown.

And in this forest, a barbed memory
shrills like a horn; my blood cells start to roar.
I think of sailors shipwrecked on a reef,
convicts, broken poets and many more.

ROUND AND ROUND

A single red car's a sun in the mist;
the sixties music played in the nineties
soft-focuses such different decades.

The driver's looking for the yellow house
at Arles. His girlfriend paints a red toe-nail,
holding her left foot in her hand.
The oaks are heavy. Acorn flurries hit the car.

He thought he had a passenger,
but it's more the idea preoccupies.
Faces are never fixed, their dimensions

go inside and come back at us
when we least expect it. They reappear
like self-inflatable balloons.
Eyes, a mouth, or no eyes and no mouth.

The house is lost in mist. He drives around.
He doesn't want to know she isn't there.
Autumn is yellow on the ground.

An empty screen. A rectangle of fog
concedes to figures running – Polish refugees?
A montage of historical fragments
explodes in black and white. Napoleon

confronting Salvador Dali?
Then endless birches on a Russian plain.
A mobile of suspended glass trinkets
on the black window alerts me to rain.

The night outside instates its dialogue.
A whiplash branch, a big hum in the sky.
The camera finds among convergent points
faces of those who have already had to die . . .

I'm displaced, a black cat curls up
beside me on a green cushion. His stare
takes in what I can't see,
something which came before me and is still out there.

LOSS

We came back: hands open to receive light
for the black diagram mapped in our palms.

A lifetime we had looked for the vision:
moonlight painting a black canvas;
filigree features
of the unknown one.

We had forgotten why this dusty square
claimed us. One white wall splashed with blood.

We grouped around our loss.
An absence that went black and deep as space
and went on falling
through

our hands. We knew why we had come.

I closed the night inside a book,
its blackness illuminated by gold,
and when I came back to the page
my thinking had altered the words,

changed the dance steps, a new rhythm
touched the moving points; a voyage begun
under a red-gold sun.
My night would never be the same,
and repetition of the act
created variations of a game,

the Name, the Name
eluded me;

and other preoccupations, geese gone
over in the dark, a taxi
reassuringly cruising through blue rain,
conveying two to a black tented bed,
he dressed in white and she in red

to lie in one window of flesh.
Black death-ships in the words, and flame
beaconing from a high summit,

the Name, the Name
was in the journey. I have counted nights,
the singe-marks around lettering,
the red wax seal on history, the flights

into the brief transition of the day.

A state of apprehension. A flatland
in which I have no language – 26
letters went over like death-birds

migrating to a black desert.
I had to be transparent, had to find
the 27th, the directing Word,
the ongoing who'd make me visible
within his mirror. Look, I am no-one
returning to someone.
A rainbow arching from the sand.

Nothing that I'd imagined;
no jade sphinx nor blue jackal,
no crowds stopped at an oasis,
instructors pointing the way,
community nor expression.

There were oil-stains, libraries written in sand
and a circle I kept walking,
white with a red eye in the centre,

a circle I'd never enter.

BREAD

Stars, and the morning smell of bread.
We were waiting for this dispensation,
blue as it comes back, red

as it goes; the continuity
of whatever the dark had broken off.
In my dream landscape there were pyramids,
an orange sun with wings, a purple sail
on the green Nile.
                              Later the void.

Today I think of Rimbaud's delirium:
hunger-pains, his stealing down, hallucinated,
to buy bread hot from the oven,
Paris still dark, the urgent marketeers.
The warm stick cradled in his hands,
his attic musty with dope smells.

Bread, ink and wine. The visionary sands
folding wings over hunger,
dreaming of a blue rose flowering in dust
and dust turning to flesh on blackened hands.

The man of vision at the end of time,
he writes his name, the Name in ash on dust,
a logogram to be re-ordered by the wind,
given back to the void.
                          The sky in flames.

He passes an eroded car; two tail to tail
as though seeking comfort
in being inanimate.
The open field-gate
leads nowhere. If he would speak it's to himself;

and out of that the discourse would establish
a shadow with a mouth that speaks,
the first stage to a new species.

Blue thistles by the wall, hairy nettles.
These have survived. He looks for little things
to reconstitute memory.

I am this one, I was that one,
the things I needed they are gone
to blacken in the sun.

A tape-loop clicks to a terminal halt.
The trompe l'œil landscape improvised on the window
finds its reverse outside. A little girl
stands reading beneath a mountain –
a red sun balanced on its cobalt peak.
She's come without fear to this place. Naive
blue flowers are implanted in the grass.
Those looking up can see it too:
a narrative imposed on a white wall.

The person inside leaves by a back door
into another world. The speeches he dictates
are discoveries he commits to burial.
Ghost-written archives for a president
come here from another planet. Someone
who needs his policy
validated by these discoveries?

He's rarely seen. Committing history
to audios, driving a shaded car
towards his own recording studio.
He's silent, and the story's come this far.

BABEL

Stone flighted conically towards the sky –
a word-tower extending from a poet's mouth
to the sun; vision the dream of language

and its dispersal.
And always the vibration: the seamless word
alive to the animals under trees,
the river directed by the salmon's dictates,
flowers instructed as lovers by bees.

And whether of stone or light it stood, and
they came across deserts to hear
the universal resonance.

When the poet couldn't sustain the dream
it crashed. Light was translated back to stone
and the fall smashed a hollow
in the earth; thunder reverberated.
The animals fled and were individualised –

and those tribes who survived the shock
ran and articulated screams
and each recognised their disunity –
brother and sister and lover

and were never again one when they spoke to each other.

WHITE HORSES
for Alan Clodd

Climb with the equinox from a green bay,
surf-horses, high-maned, wind-driven, white-plumed,
step ashore on the mirrored sand,
blue-eyed Atlantic horses, caracole
in the backwash, return to the sea-plains,
a threshed blue-black pampa, a brackish shoal
spined with white water, strophe and antistrophe;
I bring you news of tides, for poetry
lives in that rhythm, violet, peacock, grey
thalassic odes – it's the voice of the sea
sounds in Neruda, Lorca, St-John Perse,
the universal lyric, dazzling spray
from the antipodes and always white
stallions thundering for the shore.
The years too are like sea-smoke – look behind
and we're no longer where we thought we were,
not here, not there, but hurried by the tide
towards a look-out post, illusory
sea-mark, but all we have against the flux,
the greater sea within.
                              I bring you late roses,
full-skirted, scarlet, richer for the gold summer,
marine roses to place for white horses
under green moonlight on this beach
where waves in cadence measure out their reach.